Meet NASA Inventor Chang-kwon Kang and His Team's

Mars-Exploring Flying Swarm

WORLD
BOOK

www.worldbook.com

World Book, Inc.
180 North LaSalle Street
Suite 900
Chicago, Illinois 60601
USA

For information about other World Book publications, visit our website at www.worldbook.com or call 1-800-WORLDBK (967-5325).

For information about sales to schools and libraries, call 1-800-975-3250 (United States), or 1-800-837-5365 (Canada).

Produced in collaboration with the National Aeronautics and Space Administration (NASA).

Library of Congress Cataloging-in-Publication Data for this volume has been applied for.

Out of This World
ISBN: 978-0-7166-6261-7 (set, hc.)

Mars-Exploring Flying Swarm
ISBN: 978-0-7166-6266-2 (hc.)

Also available as:
ISBN: 978-0-7166-6274-7 (e-book)

Printed in USA by Corporate Graphics
1st printing May 2021

Staff

Editorial

Director
Tom Evans

Manager
Jeff De La Rosa

Writer
William D. Adams

Proofreader
Nathalie Strassheim

Graphics and Design

Senior Visual
Communications Designer
Melanie Bender

Media Researcher
Rosalia Bledsoe

Acknowledgments

Cover	NASA/JPL-Caltech; Chang-kwon Kang; © Omnart/Shutterstock	32-33	NASA; Chang-kwon Kang
4-7	© Shutterstock	34-35	© Irina Kuzmina, Shutterstock
8-9	© Mark Garlick, Science Photo Library/Getty Images	37	NASA/JPL-Caltech/MSSS
10-11	NASA/JPL	38-39	© Chesky/Shutterstock
12-13	© Adcharatt Suwanpugdee, Shutterstock	40-41	© SCIEPRO/Getty Images; Chang-kwon Kang
14	© Fred Stein Archive/Archive Photos/Getty Images	43-44	Chang-kwon Kang
16-17	© Jayjued/Shutterstock		
18-19	NASA/JPL-Caltech		
20-21	Chang-kwon Kang; © Frank Cornelissen, Shutterstock		
23	© Paul Taggart, Bloomberg/Getty Images		
24-27	© Shutterstock		
28-29	Ben Finio, The Harvard Microrobotics Lab		
30-31	Chang-kwon Kang; © JHVEPhoto/Shutterstock		

Contents

Glossary There is a glossary of terms on page 45. Terms defined in the glossary are in boldface type that **looks like this** on their first appearance on any spread (two facing pages).

Pronunciations (how to say words) are given in parentheses the first time some difficult words appear in the book. They look like this: pronunciation (pruh NUHN see AY shuhn).

Introduction

When it comes to studying Mars, it can be difficult
to connect the details with the big picture.
Orbiters can circle hundreds of miles or kilometers
above the Martian surface, providing a bird's-eye
view of the Red Planet. However, the images they
produce may lack detail.

Rovers can study the Martian landscape much
more closely. But these rolling robots cannot travel
very fast or look very far.

For a lengthy study of most of the solid objects
in our **solar system,** mission planners have
these two choices: orbiters and rovers. But Mars
has something most of these objects do not:
atmosphere. Like Earth, Mars has air, and air
makes possible another kind of explorer—aircraft.

It is not as simple as packing up a conventional **drone** aircraft and sending it to Mars, however. The Martian **atmosphere** is much thinner than that of Earth. Put simply, there's just not enough air to hold aloft a heavy, conventional aircraft. Also, aircraft often rely on air for more than just the wind beneath their wings. They combine oxygen from the air with fuel to reach the speeds they need to stay aloft.

To conquer the Martian skies, the **aerospace engineer** Chang-kwon Kang will have to design a different kind of aircraft. For inspiration, he's looking to some of Earth's most accomplished aviators—insects. Kang envisions sending a swarm of insect-inspired drones, called Marsbees, to the Red Planet. These tiny explorers could flap about, collecting detailed information over a vast area of the surface.

Artist's illustration of Mars's thin atmosphere

The titles in the *Out of This World* series feature projects that have won grant money from a group formed by the United States National Aeronautics and Space Administration, or NASA. The NASA Innovative Advanced Concepts program (NIAC) provides funding to teams working to develop bold new advances in space technology. You can visit NIAC's website at www.nasa.gov/niac.

Meet Chang-kwon Kang.

❝ I'm an aerospace engineer at the University of Alabama in Huntsville. I've studied the long-distance migration of butterflies. Their ability to travel great distances in high, thin air is part of the inspiration behind my Marsbees! ❞

Destination: Mars

Mars is a cold, rocky, desert planet. But billions of years ago, it was a much different place. The surface temperature was much warmer than it is today. Rivers of liquid water flowed into lakes and shallow oceans. A thick **atmosphere** blanketed the planet.

What happened to that seeming paradise? Did life ever arise there? And if so, did it die out when the atmosphere thinned and the planet cooled? Or, did life retreat underground, where liquid water can still be found? Scientists look to space **probes** to help answer these and other intriguing questions.

Orbiters and **rovers** already patrol the Red Planet, and more are on the way. These craft are the tools that have enabled scientists to paint such a tantalizing picture of Mars's past. Why bother trying to build a Martian aircraft, then?

Billions of years ago,
Mars likely had liquid
water on its surface.

Why fly the Martian skies?

Orbiting satellites give a broad view of the entire Martian surface. The National Aeronautics and Space Administration (NASA) Mars Reconnaissance **Orbiter** (MRO), for example, has a special camera that captures surface details as small as 1 foot (30 centimeters) across. That's pretty amazing, but scientists would like to capture even finer detail. Also, scanning the surface in such detail takes time. The MRO only mapped about 2.5 percent of Mars to this level of detail in its first decade in orbit. **Landers** and **rovers** give an even more detailed view, but only of a tiny area.

An airborne **drone** could provide greater detail than an orbiter while covering more ground than a wheeled rover. Such a craft could, for example, scout locations of interest for visits by future rovers or even human explorers. Also, NASA and other space agencies hope to send missions to return samples— and even crewed missions—to Mars. Either type of mission requires launching a return rocket from the Martian surface.

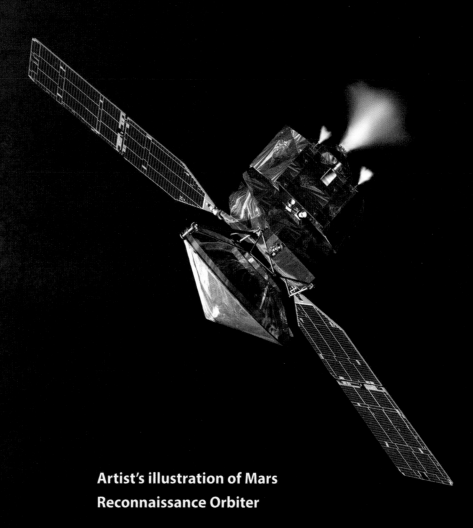

> **"** To launch a rocket from the surface of Mars, we must know more about the atmospheric conditions. A flying drone could provide useful data about air temperature, pressure, and density, helping to prepare for the rocket launch. **"** —Chang-kwon

Artist's illustration of Mars Reconnaissance Orbiter

How things fly

On Earth, **gravity** pulls everything down toward the surface, ensuring that what goes up must come down. Airplanes (and some living things) are able to "cheat" this rule by taking advantage of a force called **lift.** Lift is an upward force that counteracts the pull of gravity. Generate enough lift, and you'll go soaring into the sky.

Lift is created by the flow of air over surfaces with certain shapes, called **airfoils.** (Think of the wings of a plane or a bird.) Airfoils tend to be curved on top and flatter on the bottom. They are often rounded in the front and taper to a point in the rear.

The flow of air over the airfoil generates lift. Just how much lift depends on the shape of the airfoil. It also depends on the airfoil's surface area. The larger the surface, the more lift generated. Airliners, for example, need huge wings to get their heavy bodies off the ground.

The amount of lift generated also depends on how rapidly air flows over the airfoil. Aircraft thus require a forward-pushing force called thrust. Thrust helps push the airfoil through the air with enough speed to get the craft off the ground.

Helicopters work in a similar away. Instead of a *fixed* (nonmoving) wing, however, the airfoil takes the form of spinning blades. Air flows over the blades as they spin, generating lift.

lift

direction of air flow

airfoil

Inventor feature:
Einstein inspiration

One of Kang's heroes growing up was the German-born *theoretical physicist* Albert Einstein (1879-1955). A theoretical physicist is a scientist who creates and develops theories of matter and energy. Einstein came up with some of the most important theories in all of physics.

Albert Einstein

❚❚ Outside the classroom, I spent a lot of time reading books about Einstein and his relativity theories and quantum mechanics. It was not easy to fully understand such complex ideas, but the books that I read were written in such a way that young audiences could at least think about them. ❚❚ —Chang-kwon

During high school, Kang attended a seminar where physicists discussed *string theory,* a complex theory on the fundamental forces of nature that is still under development. Kang was impressed. He seriously considered studying physics and mathematics in college as a result.

Kang continues to be interested in the big ideas in his reading. He prefers a hefty book of philosophy or classic literature to a brisk science fiction adventure. His favorite novelist is the Russian author Fyodor Dostoevsky (1821-1881). Dostoevsky's novels, including *Crime and Punishment* (1866) and *The Brothers Karamazov* (1879-1880), feature complex examinations of the human condition.

Is there flight on Mars?

Like Earth, Mars has an **atmosphere.** And, Mars's **gravitational pull** is only about a third of Earth's, making it easier to get off the ground. Could it be as simple as sending a conventional consumer **drone**—for example a quadcopter—to study Mars?

Unfortunately, it's not that easy. Remember that **lift** is generated by the flow of air over an **airfoil.** The thinner the air, the harder it is for a craft to generate lift.

Earth's atmosphere, for example, is not uniformly dense from top to bottom. Air gets thinner the higher you go. Above around 60,000 feet (18,000 meters), the air gets so thin that only specially designed planes flying extremely fast can generate enough lift. Much higher than that, the atmosphere gets so thin that wings are basically useless. Only rockets can fly higher, relying on pure **thrust,** rather than lift.

The air density on the surface of Mars is about one-hundredth that of Earth at sea level—about as thick as Earth's atmosphere 100,000 feet (30,000 meters) above the surface. In such thin air, the rotors of a conventional quadcopter would twirl helplessly, unable to generate enough lift.

This paper airplane
would fall like a stone on
most solar system bodies.

17

Another atmospheric advantage of Earth?

In addition to using Earth's atmosphere for lift, most aircraft take advantage of it in another way. Their engines take in air and combine it with fuel. Oxygen in the air enables this mixture to be *combusted* (burned) to provide thrust. High in the atmosphere, there's too little oxygen for combustion, and in space, there's none. Rockets are only able to operate in these places because they carry a special chemical, called an *oxidizer,* used to burn their fuel.

Flight on Mars is possible, but it will take a specially designed aircraft to fly in the planet's challenging **atmospheric** conditions. Such an aircraft could generate enough **lift** to fly if it produced lots of **thrust.** But, flying fast uses a lot of energy. There isn't nearly enough oxygen in Mars's atmosphere to run conventional aircraft engines. Instead, a Martian aircraft would have to use powerful rockets to speed through the atmosphere. But what's the point of flying so fast? Scientists would like to use an aircraft to get a good look at the surface of Mars, not speed over it.

The other way to generate more lift is used to use a larger **airfoil**—much larger, in the case of Mars. Two **prototype** Martian flyers take this approach. The first, an airplanelike craft called Prandtl-m, consists of a huge flying wing with a tiny **payload** (the scientific instruments and other working parts of the probe).

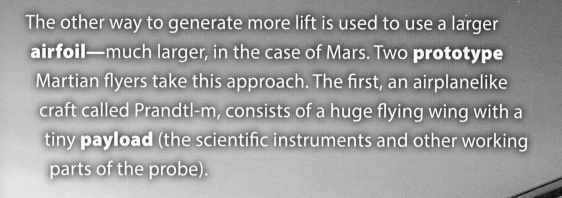

Artist's illustration of the helicopter Ingenuity, with Mars 2020 rover Perseverance in the background

The second prototype is a small helicopter called Ingenuity. Ingenuity landed with the Mars 2020 **rover** Perseverance. It has large rotor blades and a small payload, but it can only fly for a few minutes at a time.

Inventor feature:

Flying into aerospace engineering

" Among my relatives, I don't have anyone who is an **engineer** or a scientist. But for some reason, when I was in middle school, I got very interested in math and physics. **"** —Chang-kwon

Kang grew up in the Netherlands, but his parents were from Korea. The family traveled back and forth by air frequently to visit relatives. The young Kang became fascinated by airplanes and decided to pursue a career in **aerospace engineering.**

Delft University
of Technology

" I could not see how these aerodynamic forces can be generated
to fly for such long distances for 10 or 15 hours. " —Chang-kwon

Kang earned bachelor's and master's degrees in aerospace
engineering from Delft University of Technology in the Netherlands.
He traveled to the United States to complete his Ph.D.
degree at the University of Michigan in Ann Arbor.
His advisor there was studying **bioinspired** flapping
vehicles—vehicles that fly like birds and insects,
rather than airplanes and helicopters. Kang began
researching this topic as well.

Big idea:
Bioinspired design

Airplanes and helicopters aren't the only things that fly. Animals have been flying for hundreds of millions of years. They don't use spinning propellers or powerful engines. Instead, the flapping of their wings provides both **thrust** and **lift.** An animal can adjust the amount of each through small changes in its wingbeats.

A gnat looks much different than an eagle. It flies differently, too. Things with small **masses** interact differently with the air. Insects and small birds can create and ride tiny spinning rings of air called **vortices** (singular, vortex). Vortices are not very effective in helping a large bird much, let alone an airplane. But they provide much of the lift for nature's smallest flyers.

Engineers are designing smaller and smaller **drones.** Such tiny drones are called *micro aerial vehicles,* or MAV's. Like insects and small birds, MAV's with flapping wings can

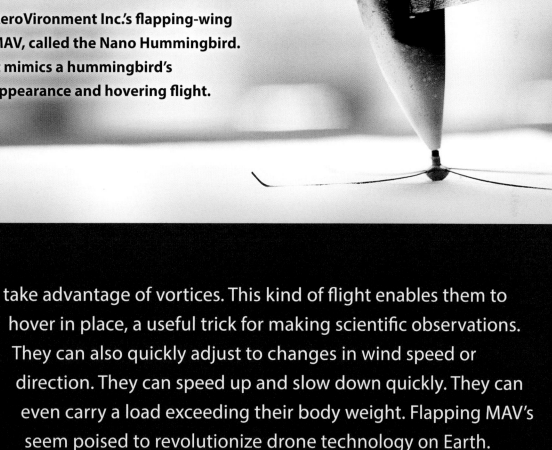

> **❚❚** Our idea is to use this concept to enhance the performance of a flight vehicle on Mars. **❚❚** —Chang-kwon

AeroVironment Inc.'s flapping-wing MAV, called the Nano Hummingbird. It mimics a hummingbird's appearance and hovering flight.

take advantage of vortices. This kind of flight enables them to hover in place, a useful trick for making scientific observations. They can also quickly adjust to changes in wind speed or direction. They can speed up and slow down quickly. They can even carry a load exceeding their body weight. Flapping MAV's seem poised to revolutionize drone technology on Earth.

A closer look at animal flight

Flapping wings generate **lift** during the phase of the wingbeat in which the wing moves downward. This phase is called the *downstroke*.

However, the wing must also come back up to prepare for the next beat. Wings return to their highest position in the phase called the *upstroke*. Flapping wings can generate negative lift during the upstroke—pushing the animal downward!

Flying animals have different ways of minimizing negative lift during the upstroke. Many birds, for example, pull their wings close to their body during the upstroke. This reduces the amount of negative lift they produce.

Insects can't pull in their wingtips like birds can. Instead, an insect's wingtip traces out a figure eight path in the air. The wing produces much negative lift during the upstroke. But the upstroke also produces great **thrust,** helping the insect to perform agile maneuvers.

Big idea:
flexible wings

Bird wings and insect wings have one thing in common—they aren't rigid like the wings of an airplane.

❝ All insect and bird wings are flexible. They *deform* (change shape) quite easily, especially when they flap. The flapping motion combined with the flexibility can further enhance **lift. ❞** —Chang-kwon

Though insects can't fold their wings during flight, their wings can still flex. This flexibility plays an important role in flight.

Flying insects have two different muscle attachments at or near the base of the wing. These muscles can flex differently, changing the shape of the wing. During the upstroke, for example, the leading edge of the wing raises more than the trailing edge of the wing. This angle of attack minimizes negative lift and maximizes **thrust.**

Flexible, flapping wings can also produce and take advantage of **vortices,** the tiny swirls of air that help make insect flight so efficient. This advantage enables them to generate more lift than do rigid wings with the same amount of power.

❝ Flapping wings can reduce the power requirement significantly. ❞
—Chang-kwon

Each of Kang's Marsbee **probes** will need this power savings to get its tiny instrument payload off the ground.

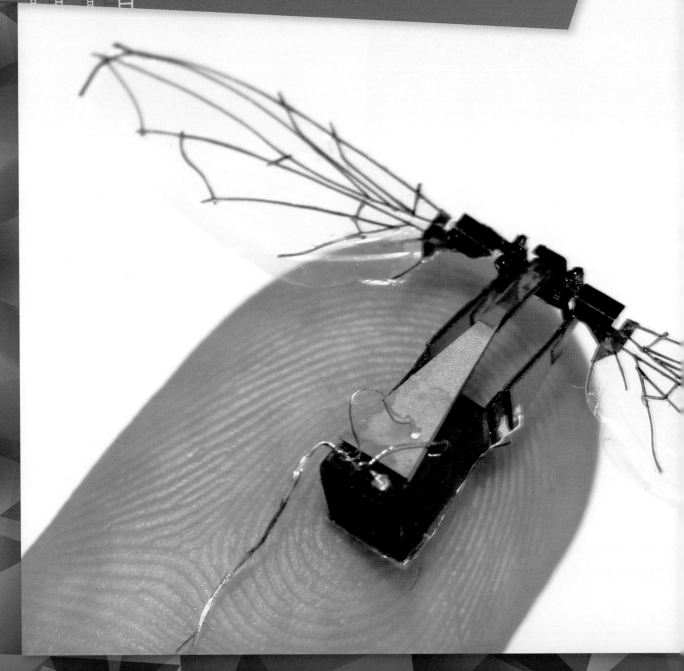

Down to Earth:

Ideas from space that could serve us on our planet.

Flexible wing technology is on the verge of revolutionizing aviation. **Bioinspired** MAV's may soon track land use and spy on our enemies. These little **drones** will use flexible wings to get the most out their tiny actuators (the devices that move the wings). Wings with flexible flaps and rudders could also enable larger aircraft to fly more quietly and efficiently.

❚❚ It's not just about flying. This fundamental concept can also be applied to swimming. ❚❚ —Chang-kwon

Flexible wing technology may make possible a whole new generation of efficient, stealthy watercraft.

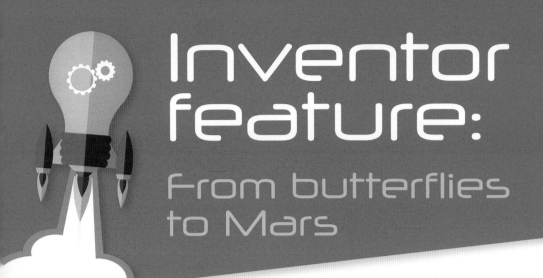

Inventor feature:
From butterflies to Mars

Kang has long been interested in the science of flight—called aeronautics—but not necessarily in space exploration. Two important conversations launched his journey into the development of the Marsbee **probe.**

Kang has studied the migration of monarch butterflies. The monarch migrates farther than any other butterfly. Dense clouds of monarchs may travel up to 2,000 miles (3,000 kilometers) from Canada and the northern United States to a mountainous region in central Mexico. The butterflies migrate much of the way at high altitudes and spend the winter several thousands of feet or meters above sea level. The air is significantly thinner at this altitude than at sea level.

A collaborator of Kang's noted the similarities between the high-altitude environment of migrating monarchs and the thin **atmosphere** of Mars. The colleague did some simple calculations and found that wings similar to a butterfly's might work well on Mars. But Kang had been mostly interested in studying the flight in living things. The design of **rovers** for exploring other planets was new to him.

❚❚ I thought it was a cool idea, but I wasn't sure how it could be funded. I talked with another colleague in my department about this idea, and he told me about NASA's NIAC program. ❚❚ —Chang-kwon

So he and his team submitted a proposal to NIAC. Their first try was unsuccessful. But after addressing the comments from the reviewers, they were able to receive NIAC funding to study the feasibility of Marsbee exploration.

Stills of a monarch butterfly in flight, above; migrating monarchs, below

Safety in numbers

Artist's illustration of Marsbees with a ground-based rover

The Marsbee **probe** will be small. It will have four wings with a maximum length of just 2 inches (26 centimeters) and weigh 1 ½ pounds (0.7 kilograms) on Earth. At this size, it will only be able to carry a few basic **sensors.** A single Marsbee won't be able to do much on its own. Also, such a small and experimental aircraft could easily be damaged in a crash.

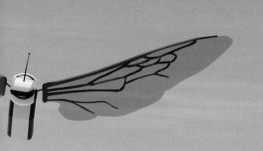

> **❝** However, because the Marsbees are going to be quite small in size, we can send a whole swarm of them to Mars. **❞** —Chang-kwon

The Marsbee probe will need a home base on the planet—a larger **lander** or **rover** to charge the tiny probe and to transmit the data it gathers to an **orbiting** satellite for relay to Earth. All this hardware would be necessary to support one Marsbee or a thousand.

> **❝** The Marsbees can collaborate with the ground rover or ground station, but also with a Martian helicopter. **❞** —Chang-kwon

A larger helicopter-type probe might serve as a "queen bee" for the Marsbees, with more sensors and greater data processing power.

Long-distance communication

Mars is our next-door neighbor in the **solar system,** but the solar system is a huge neighborhood. Mars is at least 33,900,000 miles (54,600,000 kilometers) and as much as 249,000,000 miles (401,300,000 kilometers) away from Earth at any given time. At those distances, it takes radio signals at least 3 minutes and as many as 22 minutes to travel from the surface of one planet to another, traveling at the speed of light.

The resulting communication delay, or lag, is a major headache in the exploration of Mars. Imagine a robotic **rover** encounters an obstacle blocking its path. It relays the information to Earth, which takes at least three minutes. Mission controllers plan and input a course of action. It takes at least three more minutes for this command to get back to the surface of Mars. The rover has waited six minutes to make one course correction, and that's the shortest possible lag!

Such a lag is bad enough for land-based rovers, but imagine trying to control a flying, flapping Marsbee on a six-minute delay. Now imagine trying to control a whole swarm of Marsbees. It would be a recipe for disaster.

Big idea:
Autonomy

The solution to the problem of delayed communication is to give Marsbees a high level of **autonomy.** Autonomy is the ability of a robot to make decisions without input from a human controller.

❝ We have the **engineer** Taeyoung Lee of George Washington University in Washington, D.C., on our team, who's an expert on the modeling of autonomous exploration, guidance, and navigation. ❞ —Chang-kwon

Each Marsbee will have **sensors** and a tiny computer to keep it from crashing into the ground. Individual Marsbee **drones** will also communicate with one another to avoid collisions and to ensure they are covering the area that scientists want to study.

Autonomy already helps NASA's **rover** Curiosity to perform its mission. Like other rovers, Curiosity has basic obstacle avoidance routines that enable it to move around large rocks

Autonomy allows the rover Curiosity to perform more scientific observations.

when driving to a designated target. But Curiosity can also autonomously target and study rocks upon reaching its destination. The rover identifies rocks for study using computer vision and then blasts them with a **laser** to determine their chemical makeup. Curiosity can thus get down to work as soon as it reaches its target, rather than waiting for instructions from controllers on Earth.

Down to Earth:

Ideas from space that could serve us on our planet.

Robotic **autonomy** systems similar to those used in Marsbees could change life on Earth in ways we can only begin to imagine. Think about **drones.** Today, almost all drones are piloted remotely by a person on the ground. But autonomous drones could navigate the skies in much greater numbers, making deliveries and inspecting infrastructure with little help from humans.

Groups of drones could collaborate in swarms, too, just like Kang's Marsbees. Already, artists have used drone swarms to create spectacular light shows. Such swarms may soon perform more useful work, for example studying wildlife, attacking enemy aircraft, or fertilizing crops.

Testing the Marsbee

Earth's **atmosphere** is about 100 times thicker than that of Mars, so Kang can't simply perform test flights in the open air. Instead, he and his team use computer simulations to determine how different wing and body shapes will perform in the Martian atmosphere. They've found that a **drone** with a bumble bee-sized body can fly on Mars using flapping wing motions, just like insects and birds.

" We were able to show that, with the correct flapping rate and motion, the **lift** generated in the Martian atmosphere would be enough to offset a weight of a few grams. **"** —Chang-kwon

Marsbee's wings will flap 64 times per second to keep it aloft in the Martian atmosphere!

Marsbee can't leap from computer simulations straight to Mars missions. Instead, Kang and his team are performing tests using a special Mars testing chamber. Air is removed from the chamber and replaced with a simulated Martian atmosphere.

Tests performed in the chamber can *validate* (verify) the computer simulations. If the test results from several wing configurations match those seen in the computer simulations, then Kang and his

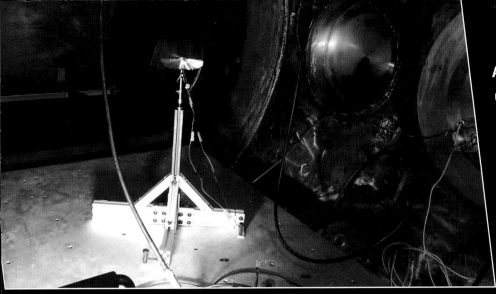

A Marsbee prototype undergoes testing in the Mars chamber.

team know that the computer simulations are likely producing accurate results.

❚❚ Nobody had shown that flapping wing motions could generate sufficient lift in an atmosphere as thin as that on Mars until our experiments. ❚❚ —Chang-kwon

Team member Taeyoung Lee leads the testing of the project's **autonomy** component.

❚❚ He's been very successful in applying his autonomous exploration methods to quadcopter drones on Earth. We're in the process of translating those methodologies to Marsbees. ❚❚ —Chang-kwon

Inventor feature:
Outreach

One of Kang's passions is teaching STEM (science, technology, **engineering,** and mathematics) seminars in schools in lower-income communities around his lab in Huntsville, Alabama. Even though these schools are located in a high-tech **aerospace** center, many students in this community have little exposure to STEM opportunities. He and his collaborator Brian Landrum have created outreach programs called Mars Madness and Monarch Madness. Kang and his lab team go to such a school at least once per year. They give a presentation on their research and engage the students in fun experiments and science-themed competitions.

Kang knows from experience that working with people from many different backgrounds helps to produce the best research. Diversity can drive research excellence through multiple viewpoints, fewer biases, and better innovation.

Applying the scientific method and engineering design process to familiar, everyday situations along with such concepts as **bioinspired** design and Mars exploration can excite kids from lower-income communities about STEM careers.

❚❚ A single event is definitely not enough. There needs to be an organized, well-structured, and well-funded effort to help these students not only to succeed in school, but also to hopefully attract them to STEM careers. ❚❚ —Chang-kwon

Kang's team gives a presentation at a Huntsville-area school.

Chang-kwon Kang and his team

From left to right: Jeremy Pohly, Hunter Dunne, Madhu Sridhar, Rachel Twigg, and Chang-kwon Kang.

Hikaru Aono

Farbod Fahimi

Rob Griffin

D. Brian Landrum

Taeyoung Lee

Bryan Mesmer

Guangsheng Zhang

Glossary

aerospace the field of science, technology, and industry dealing with the flight of rockets and spacecraft through the atmosphere or the space beyond it.

airfoil a two-dimensional shape which generates lift when air flows over it in certain directions.

atmosphere the mass of gases that surrounds a planet.

autonomy the degree to which a robot can make decisions without help from a human operator to achieve a goal.

bioinspired having a design inspired by observing living things.

drone an uncrewed aerial vehicle. Most drones are piloted remotely, but some are autonomous.

engineer a person who uses scientific principles to design structures, such as bridges and skyscrapers, machines, and all sorts of products.

gravitation also called gravitational pull or force of gravity, the force of attraction that acts between all objects because of their mass, or the amount of matter they contain. Because of gravitation, an object that is near Earth falls toward the surface of the planet. We experience this force on our bodies as our weight.

lander a spacecraft designed to land on a planet, moon, or other body in space.

laser a device that produces a very powerful beam of light.

lift the upward reaction of an aircraft into an area of less dense air flowing over its airfoil, such as a wing or rotor blade.

mass the amount of matter something contains.

orbit a looping path around an object in space; the condition of circling a massive object in space under the influence of the object's gravity.

orbiter a spacecraft designed to orbit a planet or other object in space.

payload the useful load carried by a vehicle.

probe a rocket, satellite, or other unmanned spacecraft carrying scientific instruments, to record or report back information about space.

prototype a functional experimental model of an invention.

rover a lander designed to move about for surface exploration.

sensor a device that detects heat, light, or some other phenomenon, producing an electrical signal.

solar system the sun and everything that travels around it, including Earth and all the other planets and their moons.

thrust a force exerted by a propeller, rocket, or jet engine that causes an aircraft or vehicle to move.

vortices (singular, vortex) swirls in a fluid, such as the tiny swirls in air that help insects to fly.

Inventor challenge:
Where else can we fly?

Chang-kwon Kang developed drones to fly in Mars's atmosphere. Are Earth and Mars the only two places where flight makes sense? Find your own airspace in the solar system and develop a flying drone!

STEP 1

Think about the challenge

Make a list of planets and large moons in our solar system with an average atmospheric thickness equal to or greater than that of Mars. Gather more information on the characteristics of these bodies, such as gravitational pull, temperature, atmospheric makeup, and pressure. Note how all these factors change with altitude. It might help to organize these data in a spreadsheet.

STEP 2 — Create your prototype

Now gather data about modes of flight: flapping, spinning, and fixed wings; hot air and gas balloons. What situations do they work best in? Find a plausible fit between one of the candidate planets and one of the flying methods. Perhaps you can find inspiration from flying animals in nature, as Kang did from monarch butterflies. Design your prototype on paper or on a computer.

STEP 3 — Share your design

Remember how Kang performed physical tests and computer simulations to prove his Marsbees concept. Develop a plan to test your prototype. If possible, share your design and testing plan with aerospace engineers and scientists.

STEP 4 — Grow your idea

If you were able to get any feedback from any aerospace engineers or scientists, revise your prototype or testing plan accordingly. Ask if they could direct you to the next steps to develop your flying probe. Maybe you could apply for a NIAC grant to test it!

Index